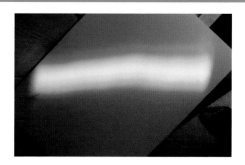

Experiments with
LIGHT AND
SOUND

TREVOR COOK

PowerKiDS
press.

New York

Published in 2009 by The Rosen Publishing Group, Inc.
29 East 21st Street, New York, NY 10010

Editor: Alex Woolf
Designers: Sally Henry and Trevor Cook
Consultant: Keith Clayson
U.S. Editor: Kara Murray

Picture Credits: Sally Henry and Trevor Cook

Every attempt has been made to clear copyright. Should there be any
inadvertent omission, please apply to the publisher for rectification.

Library of Congress Cataloging-in-Publication Data

Cook, Trevor, 1948–
  Experiments with light and sound / Trevor Cook.
    p. cm. — (Science lab)
  Includes index.
  ISBN 978-1-4358-2808-7 (library binding) — ISBN 978-1-4358-3221-3 (pbk.)
ISBN 978-1-4042-8026-7 (6-pack)
  1. Light—Experiments—Juvenile literature. 2. Sound—Experiments—Juvenile
literature. I. Title.
  QC360.C627 2009
  535.078—dc22
                            2008036886

Printed in the United States

Contents

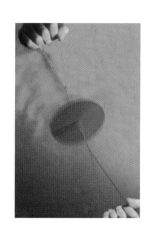

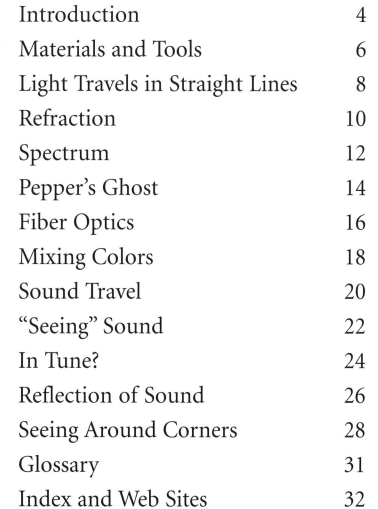

Introduction

The main source of energy we have on the Earth comes to us as heat and light through space from our nearest star, the Sun. Light is *essential* to life on Earth and not just for us to see our way. Green plants must have light energy to *convert* minerals into the chemicals they need to grow.

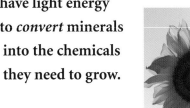

Many tools that use light, such as *lenses* and mirrors, interfere with its path and seem to bend it and make it change direction. They all work because light is very *precise* and *predictable*. Without interference, the way it travels is about the straightest line there is.

We'll look at lenses and mirrors on pages 9–15.

Ancient fortune-tellers used mirrors to make strange images appear in smoke. You can make your own *illusion* on page 14.

A long time ago, a scientist and mathematician named Sir Isaac Newton showed that sunlight could be divided into separate colors, always the same ones, which couldn't be split any further. Try a simple way of seeing the visible spectrum on page 12. You can try different ways of mixing colors together on pages 13 and 19.

Unlike light, sound needs a material to pass through. Our voices are carried through air, but sound can travel through other materials too. Look at pages 20–21 for ideas.

A foghorn is a warning for ships at sea when it's too foggy to see well. Experience proves that lower notes work best, but it's still hard to know what direction a sound is coming from. See what happens when you try to hear around corners on page 26.

Some technical or unusual words, shown in *italic* type, are explained in the glossary on page 31.

Materials and Tools

You should easily find many things that you need for our experiments around the house.

20 minutes

This tells you about how long a project should take.

This symbol means you might need adult help.

Tape We use tape to hold things in position. A tape dispenser makes it easier to tear off small pieces.

Transparent **colored plastic** It is found in crafts shops or in music shops, the sheets are often used for disco lighting.

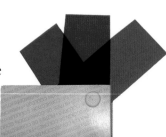

Packing tape When we need to make stronger connections, it's best to use wider brown tape.

Glue stick is mostly used for sticking paper to paper. Rubber cement is a rubbery glue that sticks most things to most other things!

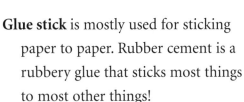

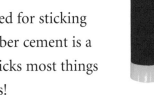

Tubes Collect cardboard tubes from paper towels or other paper rolls to use in experiments (see pages 26–27).

Food coloring Bottles of food coloring are available from supermarkets.

Scissors Ask an adult for an old pair of scissors that you can keep for all your experiments, they will be very useful. Keep them away from young children.

Plastic dropper is available from arts and crafts shops, ideal for controlling drops of liquid.

String Ordinary household string will be fine for most of our needs.

Plastic bottles Ask an adult for empty plastic bottles. The ones used for water and soda are best.

Shoe box Every time someone has new shoes, there might be be a box available for you.

Hole punch Ask an adult for a machine so you can cut perfect circles in thin cardboard.

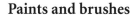

Notebook Keep a special notebook to record the results of your experiments.

Plastic mirrors are available from arts and crafts shops. Ideal and safe to use, plastic mirrors can be scored and snapped to size very easily.

Flashlight Look out for a small battery-powered flashlight, which you will need for the fiber optics and mixing colors experiments.

Paints and brushes Poster paint or ready-mixed colors are ideal for your experiments.

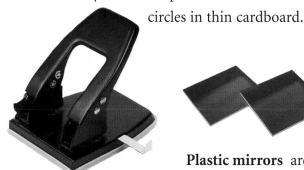

Matches Always be very careful with matches. Ask an adult to help you. Don't leave matches lying around.

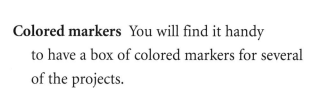

Colored markers You will find it handy to have a box of colored markers for several of the projects.

Balloon You will need a balloon on page 23.

Friends can help! Do the experiments with your friends when you can, especially the one on page 30.

Light Travels in Straight Lines

Light is a form of energy that can travel from one place to another.

The plan

We are going to show that light travels in straight lines but we can change its direction.

35 minutes

You will need:

- black cardboard, hole punch
- several different combs
- tape, flashlights, matchbox
- big sheet of white paper
- small plastic mirror

Experiment 1

1 Punch a hole in the piece of cardboard.

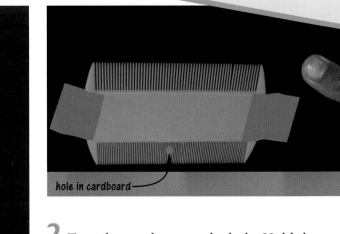

hole in cardboard

2 Tape the comb across the hole. Hold the cardboard at right angles on the white paper.

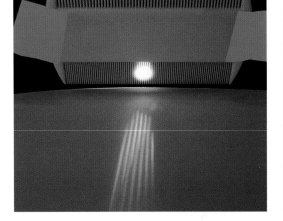

3 In a dark room, shine the flashlight through the hole, across the paper.

4 Remove the tape. See the effect of holding the comb at different distances from the hole.

Experiment 2

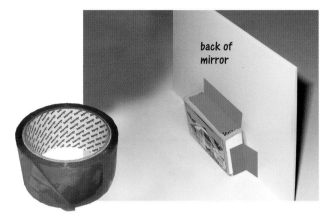

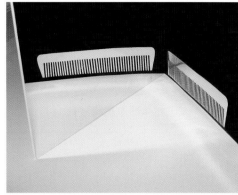

1 Tape the plastic mirror to the empty matchbox so that it will stand at right angles to the table.

2 Set up the mirror on the left. Place the cardboard and comb on the right, with the flashlight behind them.

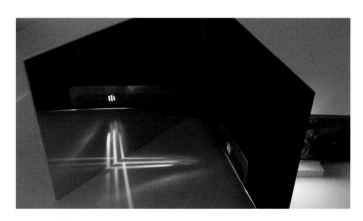

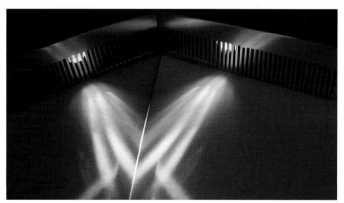

3 In a dark room, switch on the flashlight. The rays are interrupted by the mirror. What do you notice about the angles that the light makes with the mirror?

4 Try moving the mirror to lots of different angles.

What's going on?

The light hits the mirror at an angle and is always reflected at the same angle.

Jargon Buster

The **angle of incidence** is the angle between the direction of light falling on a surface and a *perpendicular* line from the surface.

5 Let light creep under the card.

Refraction

25 minutes

When light travels from one *medium* to another, for example, from air to glass or from air to water, it changes direction. This is called *refraction*. It's how lenses work!

The plan

We are going to show how refraction occurs and then make a small lens from water.

You will need:

- a friend to help you
- mug (or straight-sided container you can't see through)
- pitcher of water
- cardboard
- clear tape
- plastic dropper
- button

Experiment 1

1 Put the button in the empty mug.

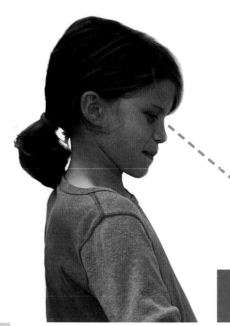

2 Move the mug away from you until the button is just out of sight.

3 Keep your eyes in exactly the same place and ask your assistant to pour water slowly into the mug. The button reappears!

What's going on?

Light changes direction as it passes from the water into the air, so the path of the light coming from the button is bent.

Experiment 2

1 Take a small piece of cardboard and punch a hole in it.

2 Cover the hole with clear tape. Rub over the tape to stretch and indent it slightly.

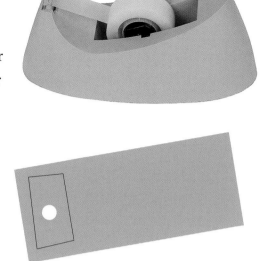

3 Use the plastic dropper to place a drop of water on the plastic tape over the hole.

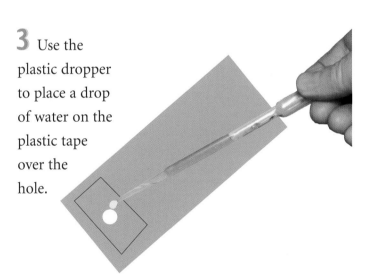

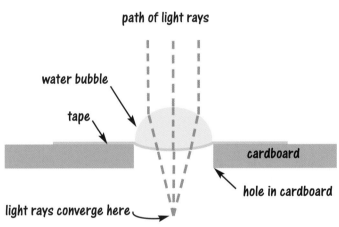

path of light rays

water bubble

tape

cardboard

hole in cardboard

light rays converge here

What's going on?

Light is bent at the curved surfaces, between the water and the air. The lower surface of the water follows the shape of the tape, and the upper surface is a natural curve created by surface tension. The curves bend light by slightly different amounts across their surfaces.

What else can you do?

Make the biggest lens you can by this method. Does it magnify any more than the smallest one you made? What do you think limits the size?

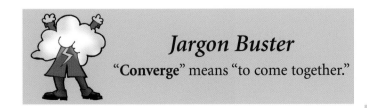

Jargon Buster

"**Converge**" means "to come together."

Spectrum

 **40 minutes**

Have you ever wondered how a rainbow is formed?
Daylight, or "white light," is actually made up of lots of different colors
mixed together, called the visible spectrum. A rainbow is formed when
white light passes through droplets of water in the air.

You will need:

- large bowl, scissors
- water, clear plastic bottles
- plastic mirror, marker
- colored plastic or candy wrapper
- white cardboard, string, colored
  papers, paints, old ballpoint pen

The plan

We are going to make a spectrum
from white light and a spinner from
cardboard and string!

Experiment 1

1 On a sunny
day, take the
bowl outside
and fill it with
water.

2 Put the
mirror into the
water and
reflect sunlight
onto the white
cardboard.
Move the
mirror around
until you find
the best angle.

3 The reflected
light should
look something
like this.

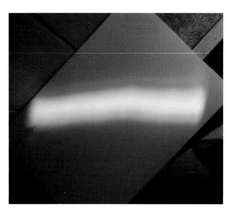

 *Jargon Buster*
Remember the colors of the
spectrum by learning this "name:"
Roy G. Biv. It stands for red, orange,
yellow, green, blue, indigo, violet.

What's going on?

Light passes from air to water, strikes the mirror and passes back out to the air again. Light is refracted each time it goes between different materials. The colors that make up white light are each refracted at slightly different angles. The result is the spectrum – red, orange, yellow, green, blue, indigo and violet. The last two are usually much fainter than the others and harder to see.

What else can you do?

Hold a sheet of colored plastic or a candy wrapper between the sunlight and the water. What happens to the refracted light?

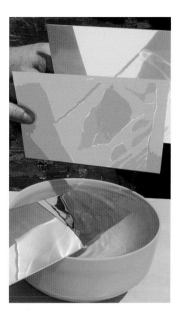

Experiment 2

 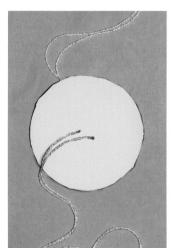   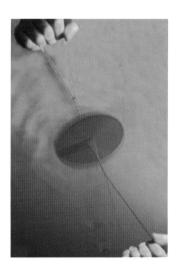

1 Draw around a lid on a piece of thick white cardboard. Now cut out the disk with scissors.

2 Make two holes in the middle with a ballpoint pen. Thread the string through and tie the ends.

3 Paint green and red on one side, or stick on two pieces of colored paper.

4 Now spin the spinner! When the strings twist, pull gently. What colors can you see?

What's going on?

Your eye cannot react fast enough to each color one by one so you see a blend of the two colors. Red and green together should produce a warm gray.

What else can you do?

Try painting the disk with different colors. What new colors can you see?

Pepper's Ghost

Here's an experiment that's part science and part magic trick and all about not necessarily believing what we see. It gets its name from John Pepper, the 19th-century scientist who *perfected* this effect.

You will need:

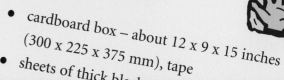

- cardboard box – about 12 x 9 x 15 inches (300 x 225 x 375 mm), tape
- sheets of thick black paper
- clear plastic – same size as one face of box
- tea light with holder, matches
- paper tube – about 3 inches (75 mm) around, 6 inches (150 mm) tall, cardboard
- glass of water, glue stick, paints, brushes

The plan

We are going to reveal the secret of Pepper's ghost.

What to do:

1 Measure 1 inch (25 mm) in from the edges of one side of the box and cut a window.

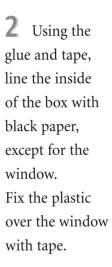

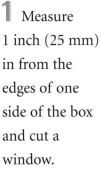

2 Using the glue and tape, line the inside of the box with black paper, except for the window. Fix the plastic over the window with tape.

3 Ask an adult to help you cut a piece out of the paper tube, about a quarter of its *circumference*, from top to base. Line the inside of the rest of the tube with black paper.

4 Light the tea light and place it in front of the box. Fill the glass with water. Find the position of the *virtual* image of the tea light and put the glass inside the box.

5 Position the tube so that the candle is totally screened from the front.

6 Now view the effect from the front. The candle should seem to be still burning underwater!

What's going on?

Usually we can see straight through clear plastic, and in daylight it appears as if all the light goes through. In fact, a small amount is reflected, but in daylight it's too faint to see.

In our experiment, we've constructed a special arrangement in which all you see is lit by the candle. We've placed the glass exactly so that the candle's virtual image (its reflection in the plastic) is in the same place.

What else can you do?

Use your box to make more "magical" effects. Create a 19th-century Victorian theater by copying the design above onto thin cardboard. Fix the decorated cardboard to the front of the box. Put photographs of friends in place of the candle and photographs of unusual places from magazines in the box. You'll need two small flashlights to make it work. Good luck! Gather an audience to watch your show!

Fiber Optics

You will need:

- glass or glass container
- water, a little milk
- plastic bottle with a screw-on top
- aluminum foil, kitchen sink
- flashlight, water, tape
- small screwdriver
- a friend to help you
- kitchen you can make dark

Modern *telecommunications* systems use light to carry information instead of electricity. How does light travel along bendable glass cables (fiber optics) if light can only go in straight lines?

The plan

We are going to show how fiber optics work.

ask friends to help

Experiment 1

1 Fill a glass container with water. Add a few drops of milk.

2 Put some aluminum foil around the end of your flashlight and make a slit in it.

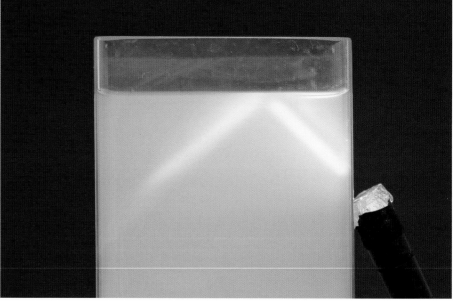

3 Darken the room. With the slit sideways, shine the flashlight up through the side of the glass, changing the angle until light reflects down from the surface of the water.

Experiment 2

1 Cover the bottle with foil, using tape to hold it in place. Leave the base of the bottle uncovered.

2 Make a hole in the side of the bottle near the top.

3 Cover the hole with your thumb and fill the bottle with water.

What's going on?

In experiment 1, when the angle between the surface of the water and the light beam is great enough, light is reflected back. In experiment 2, because of the large angle at which the light hits the boundary between the stream of water and the air, it is reflected back into the water. When it hits the other side of the stream, the same thing happens. This is called total internal reflection. The light only escapes when the water stream hits the sink and scatters.

4 Put the top back on. Keep your thumb over the hole. Turn the bottle upside down. Hold the lit flashlight against the base.

5 Get your friend to turn off the lights. Remove your thumb from the hole. The water escaping should pick up light from the torch.

Mixing Colors

We know that when we mix two different colors of paint together, we get a third one. The colors we get when we mix colored light are quite different.

The plan

We are going to compare two ways of mixing color.

You will need:

- white cardboard, flashlight
- colored paints and brushes
- clear plastic sheet in different colors – buy it from a crafts shop or try candy wrappers
- notebook and pencil
- darkened room

Experiment 1

1 Mix up three patches of thick color – blue, red and green.

2 While the paint is wet, use a clean dry brush to blend the edges of the patches together. First blend blue into red.

3 Then clean your brush and blend red into green.

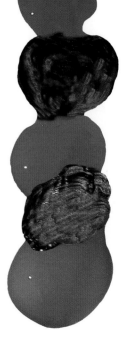

4 Finally blend all three colors together.

What's going on?

The blends between the three colors are muddy and less bright than the colors that made them. Paint is made to absorb all the other colors of light and only reflects its own.

Experiment 2

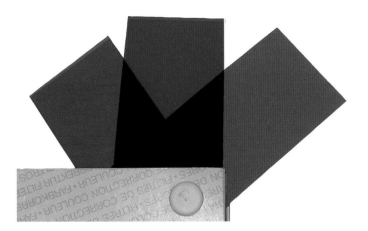

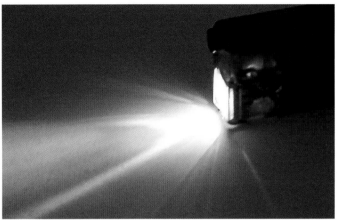

1 This time we're going to use colored plastic to filter the light from a flashlight.

2 Work in a dark room. Shine your flashlight onto white cardboard. Try the colored filters one at a time, then try combining two or three. Record your results.

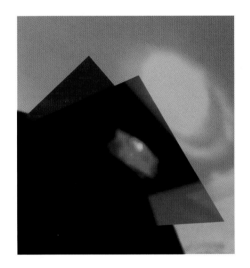

3 Try red and blue. You should see magenta.

4 Blue and green make cyan, or turquoise.

5 Green and red make yellow.

What's going on?

The results are very different from those produced by using paint. Mixing our red and blue paint produced a dull brownish purple. When we mix red and blue light, we get a bright magenta.

What else can you do?

Find combinations of filters that block the light.

Jargon Buster
A filter lets only part of a spectrum go through it.

Sound Travel

Sound travels to our ears through the air by making the *molecules* in the air *vibrate*, but it can also pass through solid materials in the same way.

You will need:

- a friend to help you
- string, metal objects, for example, silverware, coat hanger
- clean, empty yogurt containers
- hammer and nail

The plan

We are going to show that sound can pass through solid materials.

Experiment 1

1 Tie the ends of two lengths of string to objects and hold the other ends against your ears.

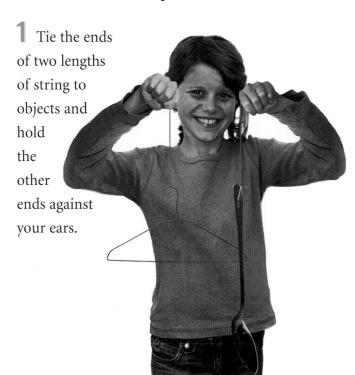

2 Swing the object so that it bangs against something, possibly a wall, or get your friend to hit the spoon with something solid. Now try using both objects.

What's going on?

When the object is hit, it vibrates, making a sound that we can hear. Since we are hanging the objects on taut string, the vibration will travel up the string, making it vibrate. Because we have our fingers pressed into our ears, we can't hear through the air, but we can hear the *transmitted* vibration coming up the string.

Experiment 2

Knot the string inside each yogurt container. Pull the string tight between them.

1 Get your string and two clean yogurt containers ready to make a great telephone.

2 Ask an adult to make a hole in the base of each container with a hammer and nail. Fix a long piece of string between them.

3 Give the other container to a friend. Stand apart so that the string is tight, and listen or speak!

4 How long can you make the string and still hear the person at the other end?

Experiment 3

Next time you are in the woods, look for a fallen tree and get your friend to press her ear against one end. Go to the other end and gently tap or scratch against the trunk. How soft can you make that noise before the other person can't hear you?

"Seeing" Sound

25 minutes

Of course we can't actually see sound, but we can see its effect!

The plan

We are going to show that sound travels in waves.

Experiment 1

1 Stretch some plastic wrap over the top of the bowl. Sprinkle some dry rice grains over the surface of the plastic wrap.

What's going on?

The sound of the plastic bottles banging together transmits through the air in waves and causes the plastic wrap to vibrate, bouncing the rice.

Jargon Buster

The **decibel (dB)** is the unit used to measure sound level.

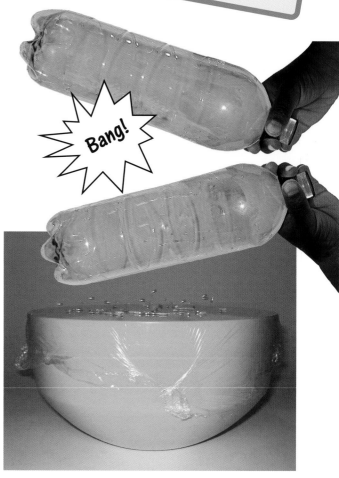

Bang!

2 Bang two plastic bottles together!

22

Experiment 2

1 Ask an adult to make a hole in the closed end of the container. We used a nail and hammer.

2 Take the piece of grocery-bag plastic and stretch it over the open end of the tube. Hold the piece of plastic firmly in place with tape.

3 Point the end with the hole towards the feathers or little bits of tissue paper. Tap the plastic at the other end sharply.

What's going on?

When you hit the plastic, the sound waves pass down the tube and out through the hole, moving the feathers. This is the *shock wave* that causes damage in an explosion.

What else can you do?

Hold an inflated balloon against your ear and ask someone to speak very close to the other side. You can feel the vibrations.

In Tune?

Sound is produced in lots of ways. Here's a method of producing different sounds using the same tools.

You will need:

- several similar glass bottles
- water, food coloring (optional)
- paper and pencil
- stick or ruler

The plan

We are going to see how sounds of differing pitch are produced.

What to do:

1 Fill the bottles with water to different levels. Put the bottles in a line. Put them in order, most water to least water. We've colored ours, but it's not necessary for the experiment.

2 Test them for pitch by striking each bottle gently with a stick. Strike each bottle in the same place.

3 Use the same set of bottles. Now blow across the top of each bottle in turn. Try and get a clear note.

What's going on?

Sound is made by creating vibrations in a material. These vibrations are carried through the air to our ears as waves.

In step 2, the sound is made by a sharp blow of the stick, making the combination of water and glass vibrate. The more water there is in the bottle, the lower the pitch, and the less water, the higher the pitch.

In step 3, the sound is made by vibrating a volume of air. The greater the volume of air, the lower the pitch, and the smaller the volume of air, the higher – exactly the opposite result to that of step 2.

What else can you do?

You can make two sets of bottles to play *duets* with a friend. One set is for hitting, and one is for blowing!

Jargon Buster
"**Pitch**" means "how high or low a sound is."

Reflection of Sound

35 minutes

Sound can be reflected in much the same way as light.
It's what happens when you hear an *echo*.

The plan

We are going to find out whether sound follows
the same rules as light when it is reflected.

You will need:

- a friend to help you
- 2 cardboard tubes (from tin foil or similar), notebook, pencil
- stiff cardboard, shoe box, scissors
- tape, ticking clock

What to do:

1 Cut a round hole in
the side of the box and
fit a tube to it.

2 Put the box and tube on
a table. Place the sound
source (the clock) inside
the box.

3 Put the other tube on the table with one end near the open end of the first tube.

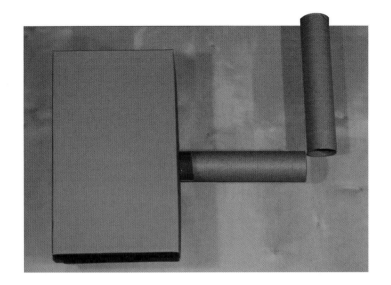

4 Put your ear to the end of the tube and get your assistant to hold a piece of cardboard where the ends of the tubes meet. Note the position of the cardboard where you can hear the clock best.

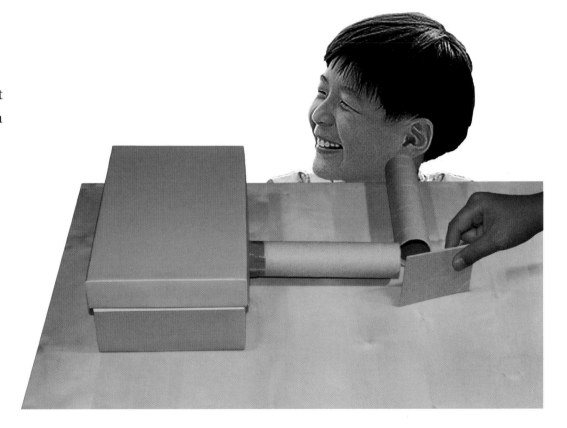

What's going on?

The sound is funnelled down the first tube and reflected by the cardboard into the second tube only if the angle between the cardboard and both tubes is the same. This works the same way light does.

What else can you do?

Try using different materials instead of the cardboard to see if some things reflect better than others.

Seeing Around Corners

The *periscope* is a device that uses mirrors to let us see around things. It's a good way to see over the heads of crowds!

25 minutes

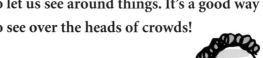

You will need:

- empty carton – clean, dry fruit-juice carton or similar-size box
- 2 plastic mirrors – each about 3 x 2 inches (75 x 50 mm)
- ruler, scissors, packing tape, marker

The plan

We're going to make a simple periscope.

What to do:

1 Remove any plastic spout and seal the box with tape. Measure the depth of the box (**D**) and mark the same distance up the side.

2 Measure the diagonal (**X**). Using the ruler, draw the outline of a square flap on the bottom of the front of the box (black line). Take care to use the same measurement (**X**) for the height and width of the flap.

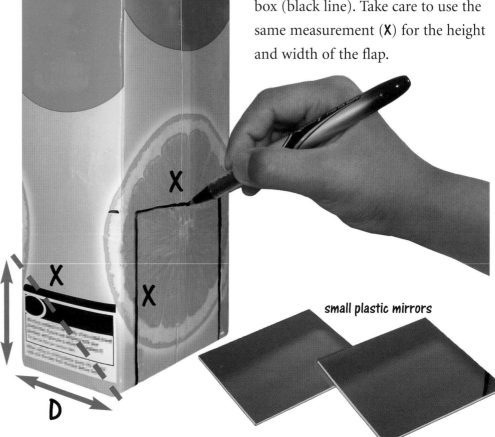

small plastic mirrors

3 Carefully cut three sides of the flap and fold it in. Use tape to fix the flap at a 45° slant.

4 Cut a flap at the top of the box on the other side, the same size (**X** by **X**) as before. Fix this flap, again at a 45° slant, with tape.

5 Stick one mirror to each flap with some rubber cement.

mirror
45°

th of
light

mirror
45°

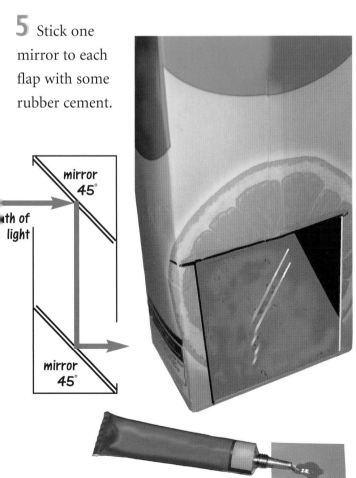

6 Now test your periscope!

See next page for how to decorate your periscope!

25 minutes

What's going on?

Light travels in straight lines. The first mirror changes the direction of the light by reflecting it, then the second mirror changes it back, parallel to its original path.

Get all your friends together.

What else can you do:

Make sure your friends make their periscopes following pages 28–29. Use colored paper to cover your boxes, and glue them with glue sticks. Don't cover either of the viewing windows! Otherwise just go crazy with paint and stickers!

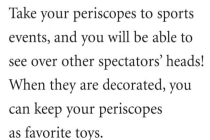

Take your periscopes to sports events, and you will be able to see over other spectators' heads! When they are decorated, you can keep your periscopes as favorite toys.

Glossary

circumference   (ser-CUM-frents) The enclosing boundary of a circle.

convert   (kun-VERT) To change something in form, character or function.

duets   (doo-ETS) Music for two players.

echo   (EH-koh) A sound caused by the reflection of sound waves from a surface back to the listener.

essential   (ih-SENT-shul) Absolutely necessary, very important.

illusion   (ih-LOO-zhun) An unreal image or a false idea.

lenses   (LENZ-ez) Pieces of glass with one or both sides curved for concentrating or dispersing light rays.

medium   (MEE-dee-um) Something through which sensory impressions or forces can travel.

molecules   (MAH-lih-kyoolz) Groups of atoms bonded together making the smallest units of a compound.

perfected   (per-FEKT-ed) Made perfect, having completed a project to perfection.

periscope   (PER-uh-skohp) A tube or box containing mirrors, designed to increase vision in submarines.

perpendicular   (per-pen-DIH-kyuh-ler) Upright, at 90 degrees to the horizontal.

precise   (prih-SYS) Exact in every detail.

predictable   (prih-DIK-tuh-bul) Always behaving in a way that is expected.

reflect   (rih-FLEKT) To throw back light, heat or sound.

refraction   (rih-FRAK-shun) Making a ray of light change direction.

shock wave   (SHOK WAYV) A traveling pressure wave caused by an explosion or a body of air moving faster than sound.

telecommunications   (teh-leh-kuh-myoo-nih-KAY-shunz) A branch of technology relating to sending messages over a distance by cable, telegraph, telephone or broadcasting.

transmitted   (tranz-MIT-ed) Passed from one place or person to another, or sent a message or an electrical signal, to a receiver.

transparent   (tranz-PER-ent) Allowing light to pass through so that objects behind can be clearly seen.

vibrate   (VY-brayt) To move with small movements rapidly side to side or up and down.

virtual   (VER-chuh-wul) Not existing as a solid object, appearing as an image or reflection.

Index

Web Sites

Due to the changing nature of Internet links, PowerKids Press has developed an online list of Web sites related to the subject of this book. This site is updated regularly. Please use this link to access the list:

www.powerkidslinks.com/scilab/light/